Geography
Revision

Lynn Huggins-Cooper

Contents

Next Stop, Newcastle!

Max, the butler, Isabella and Sir Ralph Witherbottom are driving north, to visit Newcastle-Upon-Tyne. Sir Ralph was a student at the university there many years ago.

"Are we nearly there, yet?" groaned Isabella.

"Hardly! We still have another two hours to go. Newcastle is nearly as far north as you can get in England, without shooting over the **border** into Scotland!" laughed Sir Ralph.

"Here, Izzy. Have a look on this map. See if you can find London. It's not hard to find – even on the map, the London area looks so big! Now, look for a road called the M1. It's a **motorway**, so it's shown on the map as a thick blue line. Have you got it?" asked Max.

"Yes, there it is. It's a very long road, isn't it?" said Isabella.

"It certainly is. So – here's London, at the bottom. We've driven north, passing through lots of **counties**. Now we're here, just past the Midlands," said Max, pointing at the map, "and we're approaching Leeds."

"I thought Leeds was in the far north!" said Isabella.

"Well, it is for people in London, but people in Newcastle travel south to get to Leeds!" said Sir Ralph. "When we get to Leeds, we change roads onto the A1. It's still a busy road, but it's not as big as the M1."

"And there it is. Next stop, Newcastle-Upon-Tyne!" said Max.

Label the map

Join the labels to the places on the map.

Top Tips

Look on an Ordnance Survey map and see
how many motorways you can find.

Did you know?

The M1, which opened in 1959, now stretches 187 miles from the North
Circular Road, on the northern edge of London, to the outskirts of Leeds.
When it first opened, there was no speed limit and no crash barriers. In
1959, 13,000 cars a day used the road. Today, the figure is nearer to 88,000!

Party On!

Max, the butler, Isabella and Sir Ralph Witherbottom have stopped at a **service station** for a drink and a snack.

"It's a good job they have service stations on these big roads, or we'd have starved!" said Isabella.

"That's not quite true, Izzy. We could always have left the road at an **exit** and gone into a nearby town. However, service stations are useful for a quick pit stop!" agreed Sir Ralph.

Once they were settled at a table, Isabella asked, "What's Newcastle like, dad? I've seen pictures at school with lots of **pits** and **miners**; it all looked a bit dirty and grim!"

"'Grim' is the last word you'd use to describe Newcastle! It was voted one of the best party cities in the world because of all the posh nightclubs!" laughed Sir Ralph.

"Things have changed a lot since I was last there, but the **mines** shut in the 1980s. Many men were put out of work by the **pit closures**, and the closure of the **shipyards**, and **unemployment** was very high. Traditionally, the people of the north-east were miners and shipbuilders, but now those jobs have gone," said Sir Ralph.

"So what do they do now?" asked Isabella.

"The same kind of jobs as everywhere else; jobs as teachers, doctors and solicitors; working in shops or factories or call centres…all sorts!" said Sir Ralph.

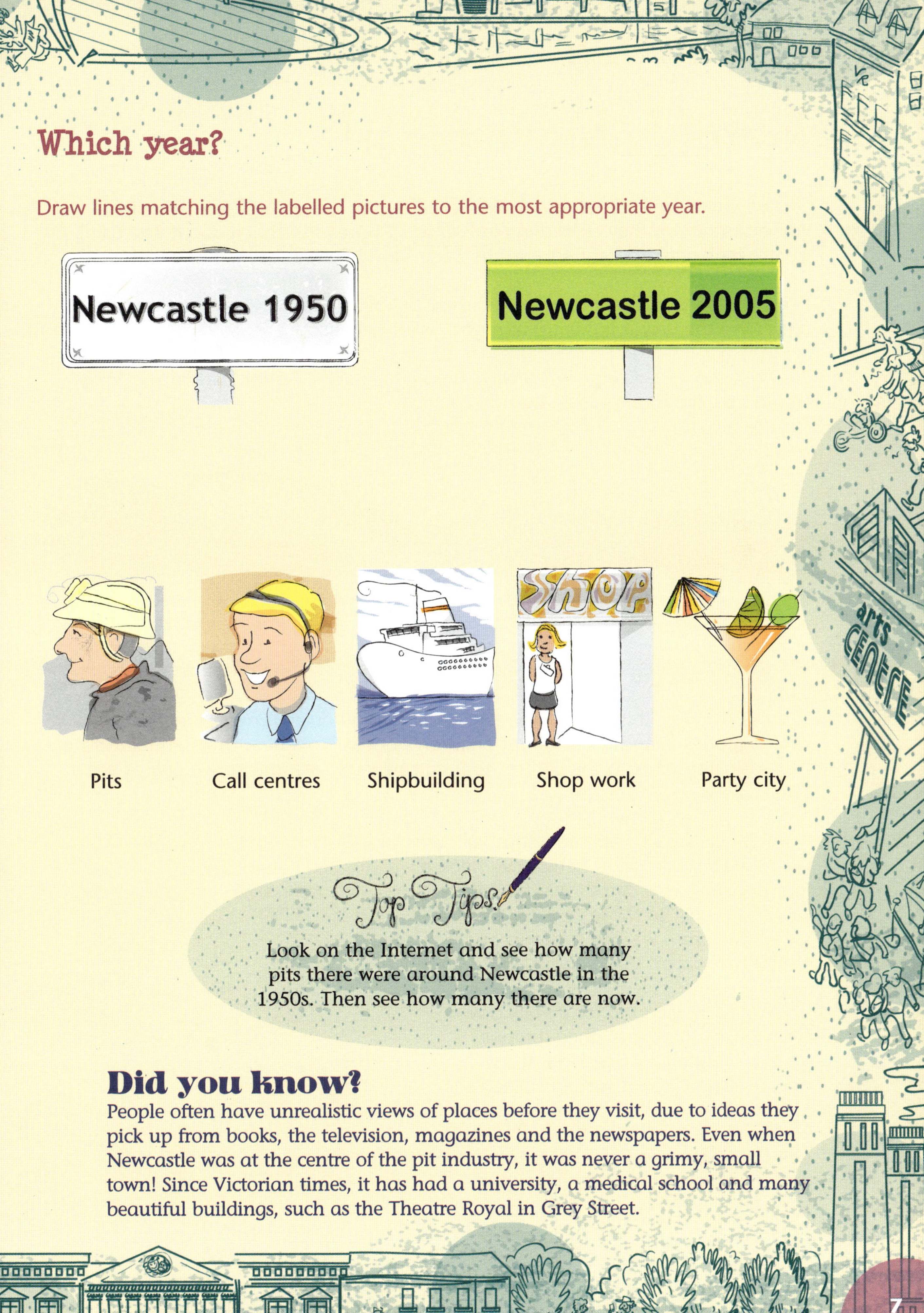

Which year?

Draw lines matching the labelled pictures to the most appropriate year.

Pits | Call centres | Shipbuilding | Shop work | Party city

Look on the Internet and see how many pits there were around Newcastle in the 1950s. Then see how many there are now.

Did you know?

People often have unrealistic views of places before they visit, due to ideas they pick up from books, the television, magazines and the newspapers. Even when Newcastle was at the centre of the pit industry, it was never a grimy, small town! Since Victorian times, it has had a university, a medical school and many beautiful buildings, such as the Theatre Royal in Grey Street.

Notable Newcastle!

"I can't wait to see all the new buildings along the **quayside**," said Sir Ralph Witherbottom, as they arrived in Newcastle. "I've read so much about The Baltic Art Centre for Contemporary Art and the Sage Music Centre. Look! There they are!"

"The Gateshead Millennium Bridge is just as lovely as it looks in the postcards, dad. I like the way it lights up at night," said Isabella.

"Ah, but the Tyne Bridge will always be my favourite!" smiled Sir Ralph. "What would you like to see today, Izzy?"

"I'd like to go to this place I've been reading about in my magazine. It's called 'Seven Stories' – and it's all about children's books! Lots of authors and illustrators have donated work to the centre, so it can be kept safe and so we can all see it!" said Isabella.

"Well, I want to go and see a football game at St. James' Park while we're here – I've been a 'magpies' fan ever since I was at college!" said Sir Ralph. "In those days, it wasn't a swish stadium – we had to stand on concrete terraces! What about you, Max?"

"Well, I'd like to go to for a walk down Grey Street and see all the fabulous Victorian **architecture** around the Theatre Royal. It was recently voted the best street in Britain by Radio 4 listeners. Then maybe go for a coffee somewhere, where someone else can serve me a drink for a change!" laughed Max, the butler.

Write a tourist brochure

Write a description of the things that might attract visitors to Newcastle. Use your description to make Newcastle sound exciting!

Go to http://www.bbc.co.uk/tyne/360/grey_street.shtml
and see a 360 degree view of many of the attractions in
Newcastle, including the Angel of the North.

Did you know?

Newcastle has a large Chinese population. Newcastle's Chinatown is centred around Stowell Street. There is a thriving community, many good places to eat and shop, and a huge arch at the entrance to the area, decorated with dragons and Chinese symbols. Every Chinese New Year, there is a street festival with lion dancers and firecrackers!

Revise Time

1 **True or false? Write 'T' for true or 'F' for false in the boxes.**

a   Newcastle is further south than London.

b   London is in the north of England.

c   The M1 runs between the London North Circular and Leeds.

d   People from Newcastle have to travel south to Leeds.

e   Newcastle is nearly in Scotland.

f   You can travel between Leeds and Newcastle on the A1.

2 **Unscramble these names of places in the UK.**

a   wecnatlse   _______________   d   esalw   _______________

b   lnoond   _______________   e   lctnodsa   _______________

c   deles   _______________   f   nienespn   _______________

3 **Fill in the missing words.**

> miners   pits   Newcastle   closed   grim   unemployment

a   People in the south used to have the idea that Newcastle was _______________.

b   In the 1950s people worked as shipbuilders and _______________.

c   In the 1980s many _______________ closed.

d   When the pits closed there was very high _______________.

e   _______________ is now one of the best party cities in the UK.

f   Many shipyards _______________, leaving lots of people unemployed.

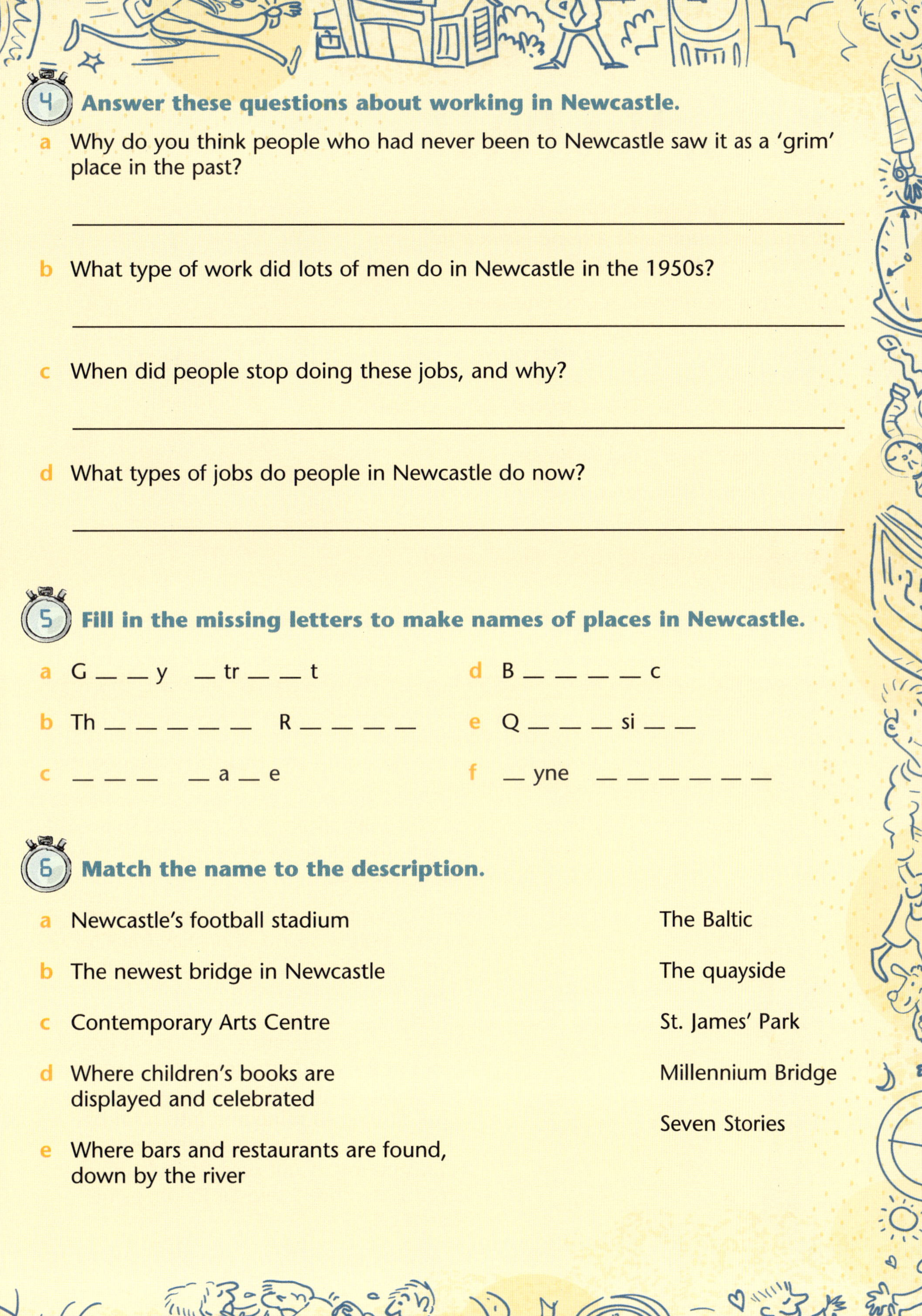

4 **Answer these questions about working in Newcastle.**

a Why do you think people who had never been to Newcastle saw it as a 'grim' place in the past?

____

b What type of work did lots of men do in Newcastle in the 1950s?

____

c When did people stop doing these jobs, and why?

____

d What types of jobs do people in Newcastle do now?

____

5 **Fill in the missing letters to make names of places in Newcastle.**

a G _ _ y _ tr _ _ t

b Th _ _ _ _ _ R _ _ _ _ _

c _ _ _ _ _ a _ e

d B _ _ _ _ _ c

e Q _ _ _ si _ _

f _ yne _ _ _ _ _ _ _

6 **Match the name to the description.**

a Newcastle's football stadium

b The newest bridge in Newcastle

c Contemporary Arts Centre

d Where children's books are displayed and celebrated

e Where bars and restaurants are found, down by the river

The Baltic

The quayside

St. James' Park

Millennium Bridge

Seven Stories

Parks, Not Pits!

Isabella and Sir Ralph Witherbottom drove out into the countryside around Newcastle to see some of the nearby villages.

"Lots of the countryside round here was changed by mines. Villages were built to house the people who worked down the pits. Imagine – whole villages where everyone was either a **miner**, or part of a miner's family! Hard to imagine these days," said Sir Ralph.

They drove on, through a series of villages.

"Did you see Watergate Forest Park?" asked Sir Ralph.

"Yes. It looked like a great place to ride a bike, down those trails!" said Isabella.

"That used to be Watergate **Colliery**; a pit! The pit closed and the council later developed the site into a park," said Sir Ralph. "There were pits all along this road – Marley Hill, Byermoor, The Hobson, Burnopfield, Dipton – and mines all over this area, with villages to house the workers. The Durham coalfields had many rich **seams** – places where coal was found in the ground – and **industry** needed the coal, so the pits were created to dig it out."

"It's amazing to think they've all gone, but the villages are still here and so are the village shops! Look, there's an ice-cream sign! Can we stop?" asked Isabella.

"OK, it'll give me a chance to look at this **wagon way** – a kind of railway track for coal carts to travel along – and the field over there at Pickering Nook had mine workings. It may have been a type of drift mine. The farmer has found lots of old bottles and jars, from Victorian times through to the 1930s, that were washed out of the old mine and into his fields. The old mine workings were used as a rubbish dump – but now the rubbish is historical treasure!" said Sir Ralph, as he wandered off.

"Well… I suppose it's worth it," groaned Isabella.

Crossword

Across

3 A city with many coalfields around it
4 This organisation developed Watergate Forest Park
5 Watergate Forest Park used to be one of these

Down

1 Places where coal was found in the ground
2 There may have been one of these at Pickering Nook

You can actually go inside a real pit at Beamish Open Air Museum. You can also visit the types of cottages mineworkers would have lived in. Find out more at:
http://www.beamish.org.uk/

Did you know?

In June 1994 Wearmouth Colliery at the mouth of the River Wear in Sunderland closed, despite the huge amounts of coal still left in the ground. It was the last colliery in the vast County Durham Coalfield to close. In 1997 the site was built on and became Sunderland Football Club's Stadium of Light.

Home and Away

Isabella is sending a postcard of the Tyne Bridge to her friend back at home.

"I'm trying to tell her how different Newcastle is to what I was expecting, dad," said Isabella.

"Well, you could tell her how different Newcastle is, compared to being at home, Izzy," said Sir Ralph.

"That's a good idea. Well, I can start by telling her about the bridges – there are so many! The Tyne Bridge, the High Level Bridge, Scotswood Bridge, the Redheugh Bridge…" said Isabella.

"That's right. We only have one bridge over our river at home, don't we?" said Sir Ralph.

"I can tell her about the lovely **quayside**, too; all the smart restaurants and bars. Did you see all the people wandering about when we went to see the Gateshead Millennium Bridge lit up in the dark? Of course, The Baltic Art Centre for Contemporary Art and the Sage Music Centre are down on the quayside too," said Isabella.

"I know – the quayside here makes our riverside walk look very quiet, but the River Tyne has always been a large, busy river, unlike ours," said Sir Ralph.

"What I like about Newcastle is the way it has all the **facilities** of a big city, such as universities, theatres, galleries and **nightlife**, but you're still close to fabulous countryside and coasts. The beaches here are as good as any you might find in Europe, with long beaches full of white sand and amazing sea bird **colonies**, such as the Farne Islands," said Sir Ralph.

"True, but you don't have to wear three layers of woollies on the beaches in the rest of Europe!" laughed Isabella. "Now – back to my postcard."

Wordsearch

Find the words in the wordsearch.

b	a	l	t	i	c	s	r	i	e	e
s	t	e	g	n	a	g	l	r	f	g
m	s	e	h	c	a	e	b	s	l	d
e	u	i	r	r	o	w	t	i	e	i
s	t	n	a	r	u	a	t	s	e	r
b	e	b	e	l	w	o	a	k	b	b
o	t	g	q	u	a	y	s	i	d	e
r	a	c	i	l	i	t	d	e	p	n
s	r	e	v	k	n	t	i	o	x	y
f	a	c	i	l	i	t	i	e	s	t

Beaches
Facilities
Tyne Bridge
Restaurants
Quayside
Baltic
Sage

Read the book 'Grace Darling, Heroine of the Farne
Islands' by Christine Bell (published by Darling books) to
find out about a daring rescue and a national heroine!

Did you know?

The Farne Islands, just north of Newcastle, are the site of the best-known seal
and bird colonies in the north-east of England. They are owned and managed
by The National Trust. Divers like to explore the waters around the Farnes
too, as the volcanic reefs are full of marine life, diving seabirds, playful seals,
and hundreds of shipwrecks.

Peace for Pedestrians

Isabella, Sir Ralph and Max are walking down Northumberland Street, doing some shopping.

"I like the way the cars can't come down here, dad!" said Isabella. "It means you can wander about, happily looking in shop windows without worrying about getting squashed!"

"Yes, blocking off roads to traffic does make it a lot safer for **pedestrians** – the people walking about – rather than driving in cars. When councils block roads off like this, it's called **pedestrianisation**," said Sir Ralph.

"It's healthier all round, of course, when areas are specially created for pedestrians," said Max. "There's less pollution, so there are fewer fumes from the cars, and walking helps to keep you fit!"

"Doesn't it make it harder for the cars to get around the town though?" asked Isabella.

"Well, it can do, if cars have to go further to get to a destination. Some shopkeepers aren't keen on pedestrianisation, because they think it can make it harder for drivers to come to their shops, but lots of people think the benefits outweigh the inconvenience," said Sir Ralph.

"Who decides whether a street is going to become a pedestrian-only area, dad?" asked Isabella.

"The Local Highway Authorities decide when they need to do something to protect an environment. This could be an old building or **restored** cobbles that need to be protected from the worst effects of traffic. They have powers to create pedestrian zones if they think it's necessary," said Sir Ralph.

"Well, I for one am glad that this is pedestrianised – it makes it safer for me to stand here and ogle the cakes in this bakery window!" said Isabella.

Which street?

Which street should be made into a pedestrian zone? Colour it red.

Look for pedestrian streets in your town. It
should be easy to see why they were made
pedestrian-only areas.

Did you know?

In full-time pedestrian streets, no vehicles are allowed access, except emergency
services. In part-time pedestrian streets, vehicles are only allowed access at
specific times. In traffic calming streets, vehicles are slowed down through the
use of speed bumps, raised kerbs, road narrowing and gateways.

Revise Time

1 True or false? Write 'T' for true or 'F' for false in the boxes.

a   The countryside was changed by mining works.

b   The countryside was improved by mining works.

c   Watergate Forest Park used to be Watergate Colliery.

d   There were no coalfields in Durham.

e   There were mine workings at Pickering Nook.

f   There used to be mines at The Hobson, Dipton and Byermoor.

2 Unscramble these anagrams about mining.

a   mneri   _______________________________

b   smeas   _______________________________

c   clloeiyr   _______________________________

d   laocsdleif   _______________________________

e   iinnmg orkws   _______________________________

f   rifdt nime   _______________________________

3 Fill in the missing words.

a   The _______________ Art Centre for Contemporary Art is on the quayside.

b   Newcastle has lots of _______________ such as hospitals and universities.

c   The _______________ are as good as anywhere in Europe.

d   The Gateshead _______________ Bridge is lit up in the dark.

e   The _______________ Music Centre is also in Newcastle.

f   There are lots of _______________ and _______________ on the quayside.

4 **Fill in the missing letters to make things you can find in Newcastle.**

a R _ _ t _ _ r _ n _ _

b T _ _ at _ e _

c M _ _ _ _ _ _ ium _ r _ d _ e

d N _ _ _ t _ _ fe

e _ ar _

f R _ _ _ _ T _ ne

5 **Answer these questions about pedestrianisation.**

a Explain what a pedestrian is. _______________________________

____

b Explain what a pedestrianised street is. ____________________

____

c Who can pedestrianise a street? __________________________

____

d Why might a street be pedestrianised? _____________________

____

e Name a pedestrianised street in Newcastle. _________________

____

6 **Write down three reasons why people might prefer to shop in a pedestrian-only area.**

a ____

b ____

c ____

Write down two reasons why people, including shopkeepers, might be against making a street for pedestrians only.

d ____

e ____

Water, Water, Everywhere!

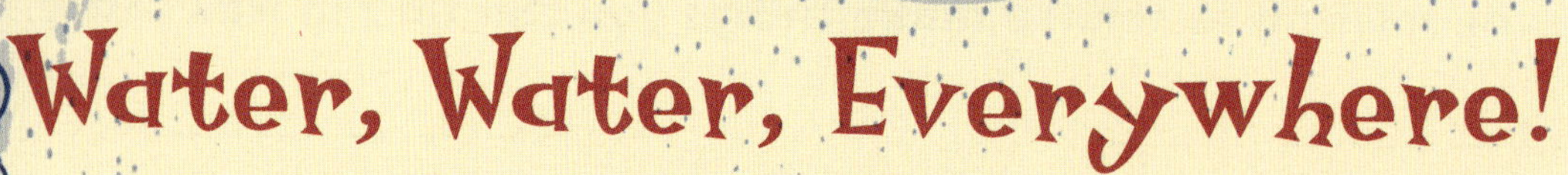

Isabella has been to the local swimming pool with Sir Ralph. Now they are relaxing in the garden with a cool drink.

"Dad, I was thinking about where water is found, all over the world. As I was swimming, I thought about all the ponds, rivers and oceans there are. There's lots of water about, isn't there?" said Isabella.

"There certainly is! 70% of the earth is covered by water – that's 326 million trillion gallons of the stuff!" said Sir Ralph.

"That's incredible, dad!" said Isabella.

"Oh, yes – the oceans alone are huge. Ninety-eight per cent of the water on the planet is in the oceans, which means it's salty and we can't drink it. The other two per cent of the planet's water is fresh, but most of that is frozen – it's part of the **polar ice caps** and glaciers. We mustn't forget the water that lies underground in **aquifers** – rock formations that store or transmit water – or in wells!" said Sir Ralph.

"That doesn't leave much for the rivers and lakes, dad!" said Isabella.

"You're right, Izzy – only 0.036 per cent of the planet's total water supply is found in lakes and rivers!" said Sir Ralph.

"How can that be true?" asked Isabella. "It looks like a lot to me!"

"That's because it is a lot – it's still thousands of trillions of gallons, Izzy!" said Sir Ralph. "Well, all this talking about water has made me thirsty. I'm off to make a pot of tea!"

Wordsearch

Find the words in the wordsearch.

Aquifer

Glacier

Polar

Gallons

Ocean

Wells

s	l	l	e	w	v	d	a	g	e	h
s	o	e	g	n	a	g	l	r	g	g
b	o	c	b	t	r	l	a	s	a	m
e	u	i	e	r	o	w	t	i	l	r
t	n	a	r	a	a	b	s	e	l	e
b	e	b	a	l	n	o	a	k	o	f
r	e	i	c	a	l	g	i	d	n	i
r	a	c	i	l	i	t	d	e	s	u
b	r	a	v	c	n	t	i	o	y	q
p	o	l	a	r	n	t	i	o	t	a

Look at a photo of the earth
from space – all that blue on
the surface is water!

Did you know?

Scientists from the British Antarctic Survey (BAS) say that over 13,000 sq km of sea ice in the Antarctic Peninsula has melted during the last 50 years. Several large chunks of the Antarctic ice sheet have broken off in the past ten years, including the Larsen A ice shelf, measuring 1,600 sq km, which broke off in 1995, and the 13,500 sq km Larsen B ice shelf, which fell away in 2002.

Wonderful Water!

Isabella was reading a book about the human body.

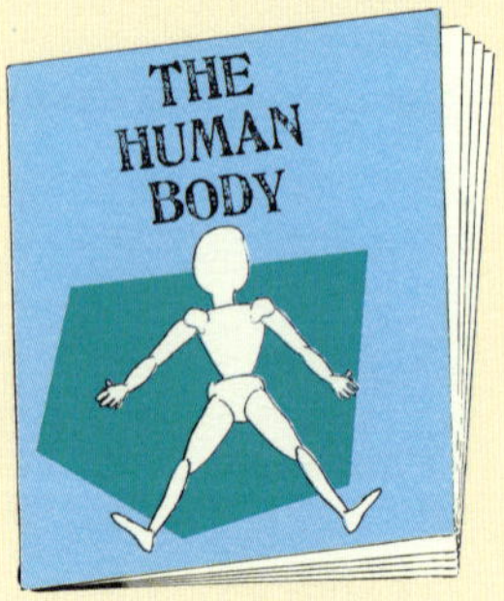

"Hey, dad – I've just read in this book that the **average** grown-up contains around twenty litres of water! That's incredible!" said Isabella.

"That's right. About sixty-five per cent of each of us is made up of water!" said Sir Ralph. "That's why it's so important for our health to drink plenty of it. We can't survive without water for more than three days."

"Wow! Is water that important to animals too, dad?" asked Isabella.

"Yes, it is. Without water, the earth would have no life on it at all – from the smallest insect to the largest elephant!" said Sir Ralph. "All living things depend on water in some way."

"What about plants, dad? I know they wilt when you don't water them enough," said Isabella.

"Plants need water too, otherwise they shrivel up and die. Water softens **seed coats** and helps them to start growing. Don't forget, of course, many creatures eat plants and without the plants the animals wouldn't stay alive, because they wouldn't have anything to eat. All **food chains** have plants in – so even meat-eating animals need plants," said Sir Ralph.

"In other words, if there was no water, humans wouldn't have anything to eat, because there'd be no plants and no animals – no food at all!" said Max. "So this lovely salad I've made for your lunch wouldn't exist!"

Number code

Work out these words, using the code.

1   23, 1, 20, 5, 18   _______________________

2   8, 21, 13, 1, 14   _______________________

3   7, 18, 15, 23   _______________________

4   4, 5, 16, 5, 14, 4   _______________________

5   6, 15, 15, 4   3, 8, 1, 9, 14   _______________________

6   20, 23, 5, 14, 20, 25   12, 9, 20, 18, 5, 19   _______________________

7   4, 18, 9, 14, 11   _______________________

8   16, 12, 1, 14, 20   _______________________

9   20, 8, 18, 5, 5   4, 1, 25, 19   _______________________

Top Tips

When the human body gives off water, such as through sweating, there is less saliva in your mouth and your mouth gets drier. This dryness is what we call thirst. It is a signal that tells us our bodies need water and we should have a drink!

Did you know?

Water is vital for our health. If we do not drink enough, we can become **dehydrated**, which can cause headaches, poor concentration and general health problems. Researchers have found that drinking water regularly helps pupils to concentrate at school. See http://www.wateriscoolinschool.org.uk/ for more details.

Water Sports

Isabella went upstairs to run herself a lovely bubble bath. Max was in the utility room, setting the washing machine and the dishwasher. Sir Ralph was in the kitchen, making a cup of coffee.

"We use lots of water, don't we, dad? You're making a drink, I'm running a bath and Max is using water for cleaning. Just think, all the **households** in this country probably use as much water as we do. That's an awful lot of water!" said Isabella.

"It is, Izzy. Don't forget the sprinklers are on in the garden too, watering the grass. We have them on a timer, so they don't stay on for too long and use up too much water though," said Sir Ralph.

Max came in, carrying a jug of mineral water with ice cubes. "Would anyone like a cool drink?" he asked.

"Yes please, Max," said Isabella. "I'd forgotten that we buy special bottled water to drink, as well as the water we have from the tap. Without water we wouldn't have those ice cubes, either!"

"There are other ways we use water, too. You like to go swimming, Izzy. We like to go sailing, and Max and I like to go fishing. None of us could do any of those things without water! Then of course there's skiing and ice-skating – the list goes on! So many different **recreations** involve water!" said Sir Ralph.

"And on that note I shall go and jump into my bubble bath!" said Isabella.

Word scramble

Take the first letter of each of these items and unscramble them to find the hidden word that uses water to work.

Letters: ___ ___ ___ ___ ___ ___ ___ ___ ___

Hidden word: ________________________________

Water is also used to provide electricity. Water power is used to turn turbines to create power. Find out more at http://www.rmi.org/

Did you know?

Factories use a great deal of water. Water is used to make paper, for example, when the wood pulp is mixed with water. Water is used to clean machinery. Factories also use water to cool machinery parts that heat up because of **friction**, as the parts rub together.

Revise Time

1 Fill in the missing numbers.

> 0.036   98   70   2   326

_______________ % of the earth is covered by water. That's _______________

million trillion gallons! _______________ % of the water on the planet is in the

oceans. _______________ % of the planet's water is fresh. _______________ %

of the planet's total water supply is found in lakes and rivers.

2 Fill in the missing letters to make words about where water comes from.

a A _ u _ _ _ _ s

b W _ _ l _

c Gl _ _ _ _ _ _ _

d _ c _ an _

e L _ k _ _

f Pol _ _   _ c _   c _ p _

3 True or false? Write 'T' for true or 'F' for false in the boxes.

a Water hardens seeds.

b Sixty per cent of the human body is made up of water.

c An average adult contains two litres of water.

d Humans can last for four months without water.

e All food chains need water.

f If there was no water, there would be no life.

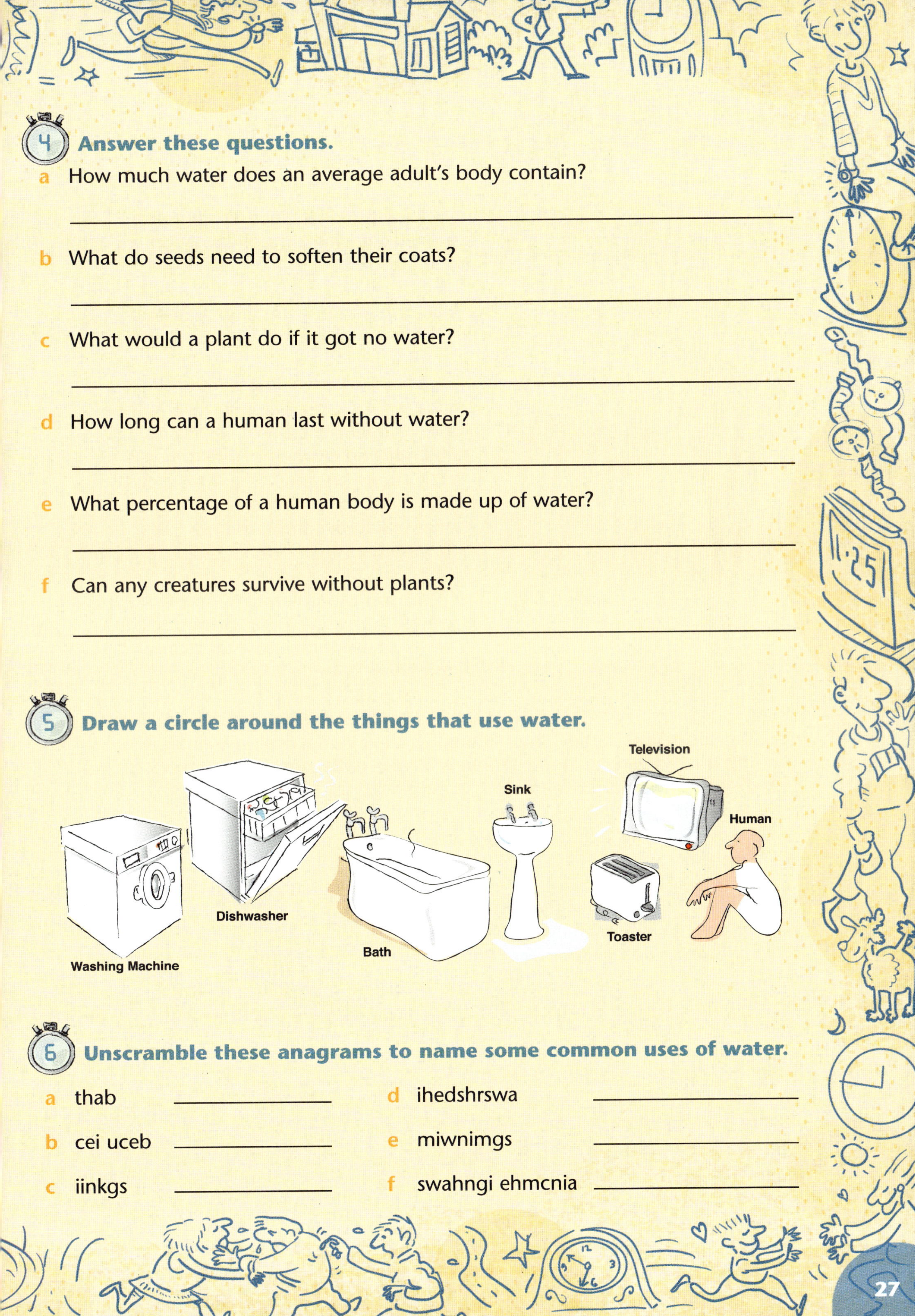

4 Answer these questions.

a How much water does an average adult's body contain?

____

b What do seeds need to soften their coats?

____

c What would a plant do if it got no water?

____

d How long can a human last without water?

____

e What percentage of a human body is made up of water?

____

f Can any creatures survive without plants?

____

5 Draw a circle around the things that use water.

6 Unscramble these anagrams to name some common uses of water.

a thab _______________

d ihedshrswa _______________

b cei uceb _______________

e miwnimgs _______________

c iinkgs _______________

f swahngi ehmcnia _______________

Clean Up Your Act!

Isabella washed her face and hands and watched the water gurgle away down the plughole.

"Dad, where does the dirty water go to?" asked Isabella.

"It runs down waste pipes into the **sewers**. The dirty water and waste then goes to treatment plants, where it's **filtered** and cleaned before it travels back into rivers and lakes. If we didn't clean water after we used it, rivers and lakes would become polluted," said Sir Ralph.

"That sounds a bit weird – cleaning the water! You usually use water to clean other things! How is water cleaned?" asked Isabella.

"Well, it depends on the quality of the water to start with. Water is often left until the **sediment** settles, then filtered to sieve out anything solid in it. Then it's treated with carbon to remove **impurities**, and tiny amounts of chemicals like chlorine to kill germs," said Sir Ralph.

"What sort of germs could there be, dad?" asked Isabella.

"Germs from animals and their waste can enter water in **rural** areas and cause disease. There could also be germs from people. Don't forget that whatever is flushed down the toilet ends up in the sewers and is pumped back out to sea or to rivers after it's been cleaned. From there, it enters the **water cycle** again," said Sir Ralph. "If water comes from underground, from **aquifers** and natural **springs**, it has filtered through rock and been naturally purified."

Crossword puzzle

Use the clues to complete the crossword.

Across

3 Another word for cleaned

4 If water comes from here, it is naturally purified

Down

1 This chemical is often used to kill germs in water

2 Another word for countryside

3 If waste water is released into water supplies, it makes them become this

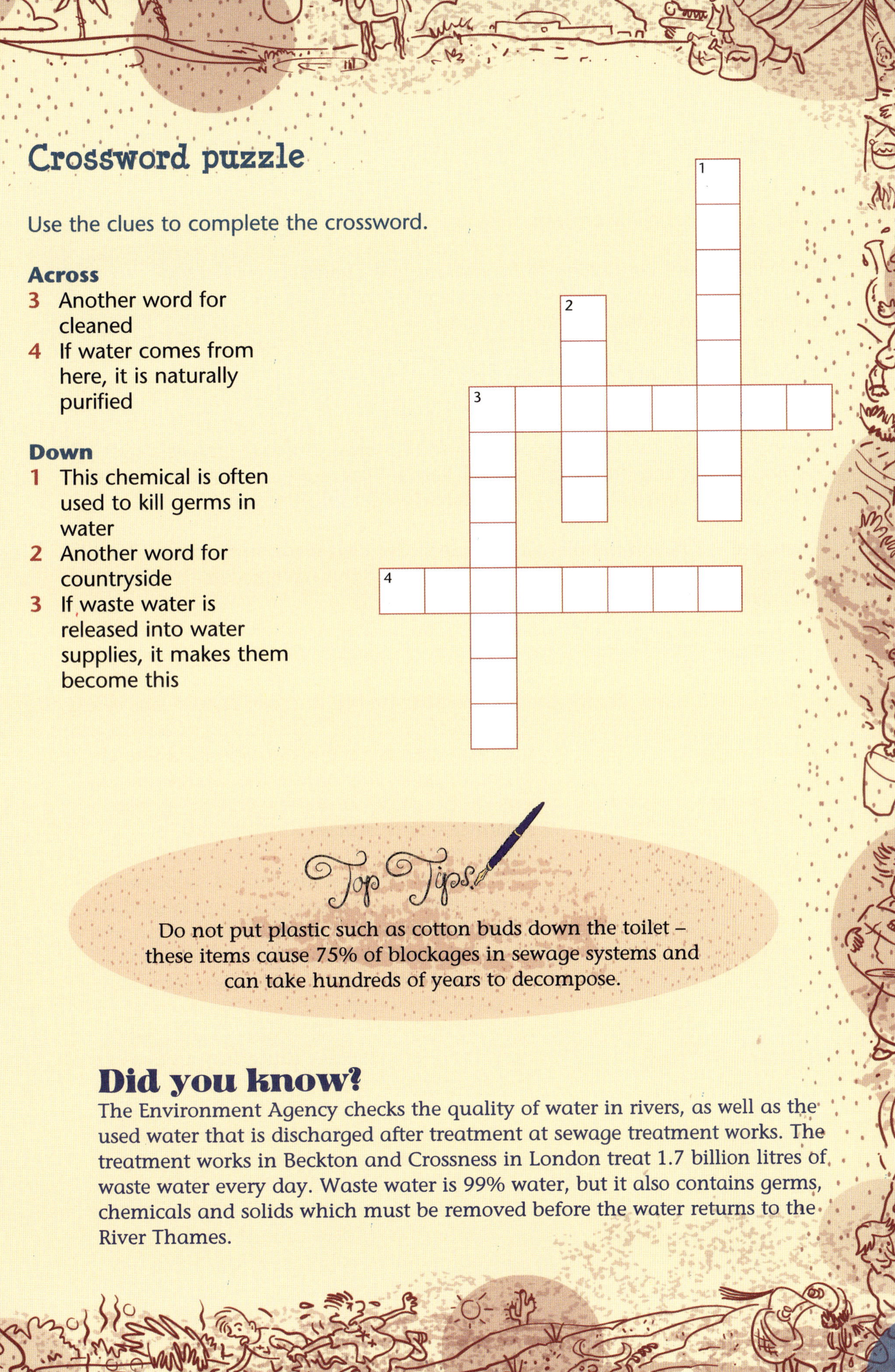

Top Tips

Do not put plastic such as cotton buds down the toilet – these items cause 75% of blockages in sewage systems and can take hundreds of years to decompose.

Did you know?

The Environment Agency checks the quality of water in rivers, as well as the used water that is discharged after treatment at sewage treatment works. The treatment works in Beckton and Crossness in London treat 1.7 billion litres of waste water every day. Waste water is 99% water, but it also contains germs, chemicals and solids which must be removed before the water returns to the River Thames.

Water Aid

Sir Ralph and Isabella were watching the television.

An advertisement was asking for donations to a charity called Water Aid, which helps to provide clean water supplies for people that do not have any.

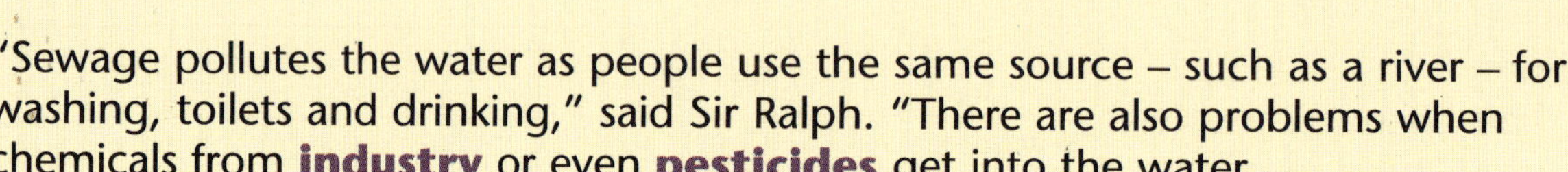

"How come the water isn't clean, dad?" asked Isabella.

"Sewage pollutes the water as people use the same source – such as a river – for washing, toilets and drinking," said Sir Ralph. "There are also problems when chemicals from **industry** or even **pesticides** get into the water.

"There are 1.2 billion people without clean drinking water and about 3 billion people – that's half the people on earth – who don't have access to toilets and washing facilities."

"How awful! Are there problems caused by dirty water, dad?" asked Isabella.

"Many! Firstly, there are **water-borne** diseases; that means illnesses caused by chemicals or germs from human or animal waste that have got into the water. These include cholera, typhoid, polio, meningitis and **diarrhoea**. 3–4 million people around the world die as a result of diarrhoea or **dysentery** every year.

"Then there are illnesses caused by **parasites** – such as **flukes**, **tapeworms** and **roundworms** – that live in and get energy from human or animal bodies. They spend part of their life cycle in water. An example is **bilharzia**, caused by a **parasitic** worm.

"There are illnesses caused by creatures such as **tsetse flies** and **mosquitoes**, which breed in or around polluted water. They spread diseases such as **malaria, yellow fever**, **dengue fever** and **sleeping sickness**," said Sir Ralph. "There are also diseases which spread easily, because of the lack of **hygiene** caused by not having enough water to wash with, such as tuberculosis."

Match them up

Draw a line to match the disease to its cause.

Cholera

Yellow fever

Malaria

Typhoid

Meningitis

1   Caused by water contamination by human, animal or chemical waste.

2   Caused by parasites which live part of their life cycles in water.

Diarrhoea

Polio

3   Spread by creatures which live and breed near water, such as mosquitoes.

Sleeping sickness

Tuberculosis

4   Caused by a shortage of water leading to poor hygiene.

Dengue fever

Bilharzia

Find out more about the work of Water Aid
at www.wateraid.org.uk/

Did you know?

Infectious diseases and parasites cause sixty per cent of all **infant mortality** around the world. Many of these are water-related. In Bangladesh alone, three quarters of all diseases are caused by dirty drinking water and poor **sanitation**. In Pakistan, a quarter of all the people treated in hospitals are ill because of water-related illnesses.

Whose Water is it Anyway?

Isabella is filling the new pond in their garden, using a hose. Sir Ralph is helping her.

"Make sure you don't spill any water, Izzy. We must make sure it's not wasted. It's good to save it because there aren't unlimited supplies and anyway, we have a water meter, so we pay for all the water we use," said Sir Ralph.

"Who do we pay? Who owns water?" asked Isabella.

"That's a good question, Izzy! Really, nobody 'owns' water in this country. Water falls as rain and the water collects in rivers, lakes and the sea. The thing is, we don't go down to the river or lake to collect water; we turn on the tap and out it comes, fresh and clean," said Sir Ralph.

"So who do we pay and why?" asked Isabella.

"We pay the water companies for water. We're not so much paying for the water, as for their services – for the water being collected, cleaned and piped to our homes, then for the waste water being taken away again in the sewers," said Sir Ralph.

"Oh, I see. People in other countries don't always have that sort of service, though, do they? In school this week I was reading about a woman who lives in the Mukuru KwaRuben slums in Nairobi, Kenya. She has to buy her water from a 'water point' in the street. It costs her two Kenyan shillings to fill a large bottle. The water pipe runs down a **gully** in the middle of the street which is filled with rubbish, waste water and sewage.

"She'd love to have a safe, clean water point of her own, but she can't afford it because it costs 50,000 Kenyan shillings – that's about £348 – to buy one and she doesn't have a steady job. We're so lucky to have clean water whenever we want, aren't we, dad?"

"We are, Izzy," said Sir Ralph. "People like that poor woman often become ill as a result of drinking dirty water. It's really sad."

Find the word

Take the first letter from each of these pictures to find the message.

____

Find out about the charity 'Tearfund' that
helps people in developing countries to
have clean water supplies on their website
www.tearfund.org/

Did you know?

The charity Tearfund believes that two thirds of the world's population will
be suffering from water shortages by 2025. They believe that 'water
refugees' and 'water wars' may happen in the future if fresh water supplies
become scarce. Scientists are trying to find a way to cheaply and efficiently
process salt water to help to avoid this problem, as ninety-eight per cent of
the planet's water is salt water – the oceans!

Revise Time

1 True or false? Write 'T' for true or 'F' for false in the boxes.

a   Waste water from houses can pollute natural water supplies.

b   It is safe to drink water straight from the river.

c   Water from all springs is too polluted to drink.

d   Water from springs is sometimes naturally purified.

e   Chlorine is used to disinfect water.

f   Water can create power by turning water wheels.

2 Fill in the missing letters to make words about water treatment.

a   P _ _ _ _ _ ed

b   Di _ _ _ fec _ _ d

c   C _ _ _ rin _

d   _ re _ t _ _ _ _ _

e   _ _ d _ _ _ n _

f   _ _ pu _ _ _ ies

3 Circle the correct words in each pair.

a   A roundworm/pig is a water-based disease parasite.

b   Polo/polio is a water-borne disease.

c   Malaria/influenza is a disease which is carried by creatures that live in water.

d   Tuberculosis is a disease that spreads easily when there is lots of/scarce water for washing.

e   1.2 billion/million people are without clean water.

f   Bilharzia is caused by a parasitic/plastic worm.

Answer these questions.

a   Name a charity which helps to provide clean water to people who do not have any.

____

b   How many people around the world die as a result of diarrhoea or dysentery every year?

____

c   How many people do not have clean drinking water?

____

d   Name two water-borne diseases. _______________________

e   Describe a parasite. __________________________________

f   Describe how water can become polluted.

____

5   **Fill in the missing words.**

| water point | gully | 50,000 | Kenya | 348 | nobody |

a   _______________ owns water.

b   The Mukuru KwaRuben slums are in Nairobi, _______________.

c   People there have to buy water from a _______________ in the street.

d   The water pipe runs through a _______________, which is full of waste.

e   It costs _______________ Kenyan shillings to buy a water point.

f   50,000 Kenyan shillings is about _______________ pounds.

6   **Unscramble these anagrams to find words that describe life in Mukuru KwaRuben, Kenya.**

a   ribonai   _______________

b   wesgea   _______________

c   eykna   _______________

d   lusms   _______________

e   asetw   _______________

f   atrew noipt   _______________

Sensible Surveys

Isabella and Max were stopped in the street by a lady carrying out a **survey**.

"We did a survey at school last week, Max. It was about **traffic**. We counted the different types of vehicles that went past the school, checking at different times of the day to see if traffic was heavier at any particular time."

"That doesn't sound very exciting!" said Max.

"Actually, it was quite interesting. We saw three fire engines with their lights and sirens going!" said Isabella. "We had to make up a **questionnaire** in food technology, too. We were trying to find out which biscuits people liked best. I could have told them the answer – it was the ones covered in thick chocolate!"

"So how did you put the questionnaire together?" asked Max.

"Well, you have to think about the purpose of the questionnaire – what it's for. You mustn't make it too long, or people will get bored. Our teacher said we should ask 'closed' questions – ones with specific answers. This makes it easier to put results together. You should limit the number of choices that you offer, or you can end up with everyone you ask choosing different answers! You mustn't be **biased** either – that means you shouldn't ask a question in such a way as to guide people to the answer you want. It was a bit difficult doing that when we were doing the survey about biscuits…"

"Oh yes, I've seen how 'biased' you are towards the chocolate ones – they're always the first to disappear!" laughed Max.

Analyse a questionnaire

A questionnaire was done to find out about travelling to and from school. Look at the results and then answer the questions below.

1 Do you come to school by:

   a car? — 5

   b walk? — 11

   c bike? — 1

   d public bus? — 3

   e school bus? — 6

2 How far from school do you live?

   a less than $\frac{1}{2}$ a mile — 15

   b between $\frac{1}{2}$ a mile and 1 mile — 4

   c between 1 mile and $1\frac{1}{2}$ miles — 4

   d between $1\frac{1}{2}$ and 2 miles — 1

   e over 2 miles — 2

3 How long does it take you to get to school?

   a less than 5 minutes — 3

   b between 5 and 10 minutes — 7

   c between 10 and 15 minutes — 14

   d between 15 and 30 minutes — 1

   e longer than 30 minutes — 1

4 Do you go home from school by:

   a car? — 2

   b walk? — 15

   c bike? — 1

   d public bus? — 2

   e school bus? — 6

1 Which is the most popular way to come to school? ______________

2 Which is the least popular way to come to school? ______________

3 Do more people live less or more than $\frac{1}{2}$ a mile from school? ______________

4 How long does it take most people to get to school? ______________

5 Which is the most popular way to get home from school? ______________

If you see people doing a survey in the street, ask them
if you can have a look at their questions. Explain that
it is for schoolwork.

Did you know?

When someone creates a questionnaire, they have to make it very clear how people are supposed to respond – should they, for instance, tick boxes, circle answers or cross out the answers they do not want – otherwise the people doing the questionnaire will get confused!

About Time

Isabella wants to ring her friend Luisa, in Germany. "Hang on, Izzy! Think about the time difference – she might be getting ready for bed!" said Sir Ralph.

"What do you mean, dad? It's not bedtime yet!" said Isabella.

"Well, Izzy, Germany is in a different **time zone** to us here in the UK," said Sir Ralph.

"What? Where's the time machine?" laughed Isabella.

"No, no time machine yet, I'm afraid; it's just that the earth is divided into 24 time zones. Each time zone is one hour different to the next. The middle line, or **meridian**, is in Greenwich in London. All the other time zones are worked out according to **Greenwich Mean Time**. Each time zone to the east of Greenwich is on an earlier time zone and each time zone to the west of Greenwich is on a later time zone."

"Wow! That's a bit complicated!" said Isabella.

"Not really, Izzy! Anyway, Germany is an hour ahead of us," said Sir Ralph.

"I'll tell you what is confusing," said Max. "When the clocks go forwards or backwards."

"What do you mean, Max? I'm confused now!" said Isabella.

"In spring, on a Sunday at the end of March, the clocks go forwards by an hour. They change back again by an hour on a Sunday at the end of October. Even the name for the clocks going forwards is confusing! Some people call it 'Daylight Saving Time' or DST, and other people just call it 'British Summer Time'."

"How confusing! I think I'll leave that phone call until the morning," said Isabella.

Number puzzle

Decode these words, using the code.

1 13, 5, 18, 9, 4, 9, 1, 14   _______________________

2 20, 9, 13, 5   26, 15, 14, 5   _______________________

3 7, 18, 5, 5, 14, 23, 9, 3, 8   _______________________

4 19, 21, 13, 13, 5, 18   20, 9, 13, 5   _______________________

5 13, 1, 18, 3, 8   _______________________

6 15, 3, 20, 15, 2, 5, 18   _______________________

7 5, 1, 18, 12, 9, 5, 18   _______________________

8 6, 15, 18, 23, 1, 18, 4, 19   _______________________

9 2, 1, 3, 11, 23, 1, 18, 4, 19   _______________________

Top Tips

If you visit Greenwich, you can actually
stand on the meridian – the middle line, or
even stand with one foot either side of it!

Did you know?

Greenwich Mean Time (GMT) is also sometimes called Greenwich
Meridian Time. This is because it is measured from the Greenwich
Meridian Line at the Royal Observatory at Greenwich, in London.
Although the clocks change forwards one hour in the spring and change
back one hour in the autumn, GMT stays the same all year round.

Time Travel

Isabella decided to make a **time zone** grid, to show how time varies around the world. Max found her a large sheet of card.

"Well, Max – it's 6pm on Saturday here in London, so I'm going to make a list of times for other places in the world. That's 4am on Sunday in Sydney, Australia... and 10am on Saturday in Vancouver, Canada... it's 1pm on Saturday in Washington DC in America... 9pm on Saturday in Nairobi, 3am on Sunday in Tokyo, and noon on Saturday in Mexico City!" said Isabella.

"It's strange, isn't it? People are going to work as we're going to bed!" laughed Max.

"I know – I wonder what I'd be doing now if I lived in Mexico City? Perhaps I'd be eating lunch, or going to the market," said Isabella.

"If we lived in Sydney, the sun would just be rising on a new, hot sunny day... and we'd all still be in bed!" said Max.

"If we lived in Vancouver, we might be going for brunch, or going on a boat trip for some whale watching!" said Isabella. "If we lived in Tokyo, we'd be fast asleep."

"If we were in Nairobi, you'd be getting ready for bed! Unfortunately for you, though, it's 6pm and time to do the washing up!" laughed Max.

Time and place

If it is 6pm GMT, then match the following places to the correct times.

1	Sydney	3am on Sunday
2	Washington DC	1pm on Saturday
3	Nairobi	9pm on Saturday
4	Vancouver	12 noon on Saturday
5	Mexico City	10am on Saturday
6	Tokyo	4am on Sunday

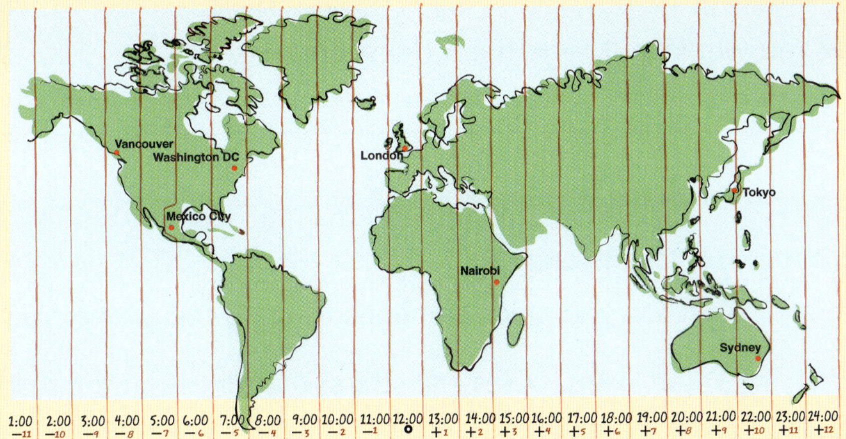

Top Tips!

Find the times for different zones
around the world at
http://www.timeanddate.com/worldclock/

Did you know?

The Greenwich **meridian** marks the starting point of every time zone in
the world. GMT is **Greenwich Mean Time**, the 'mean' or average time
that the earth takes to turn from noon to noon. Times around the world
are written as GMT + or GMT −. Nairobi, for example, is GMT + 3 and
Buenos Aires is GMT − 3.

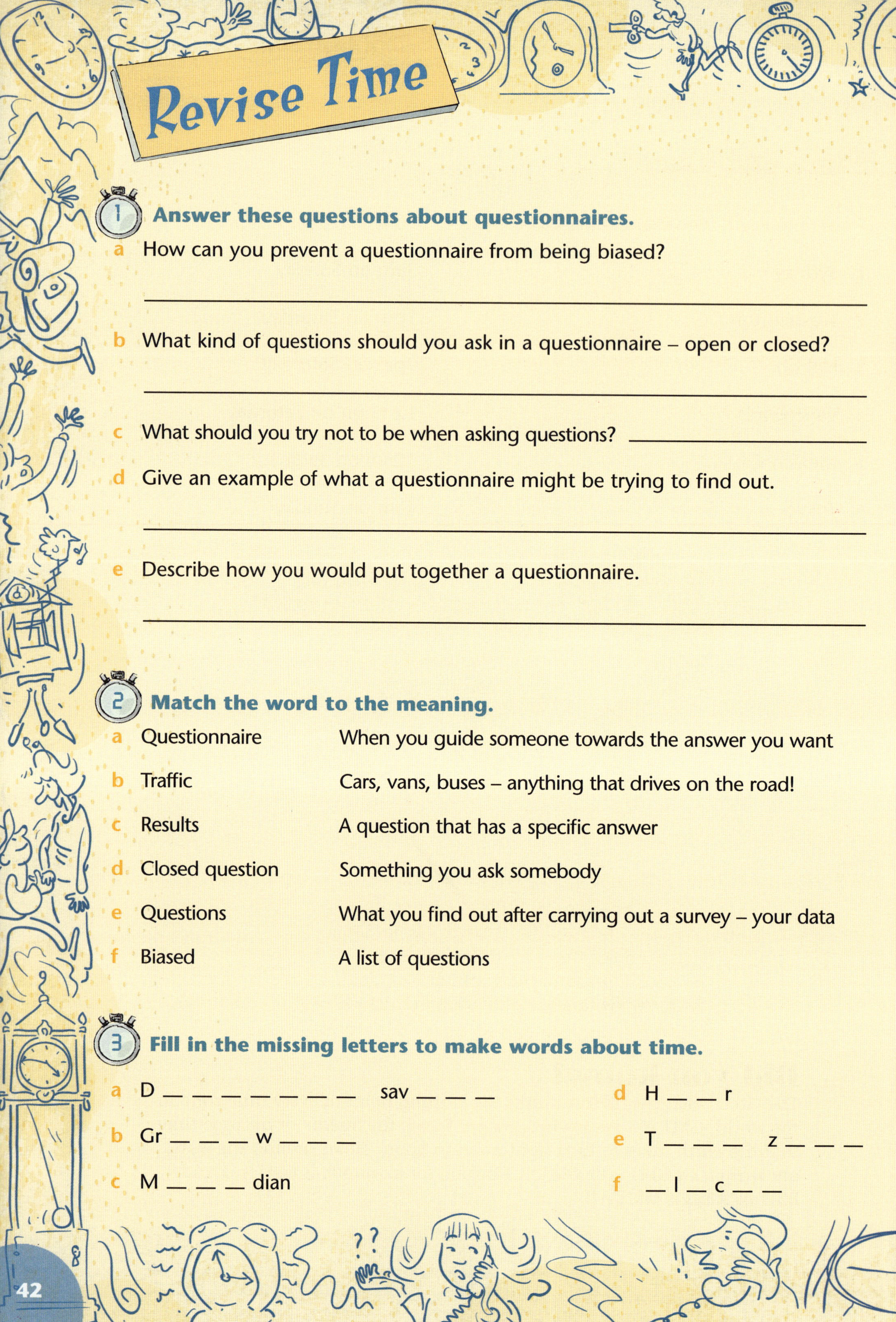

Revise Time

1 Answer these questions about questionnaires.

a How can you prevent a questionnaire from being biased?

____

b What kind of questions should you ask in a questionnaire – open or closed?

____

c What should you try not to be when asking questions? _______________________

d Give an example of what a questionnaire might be trying to find out.

____

e Describe how you would put together a questionnaire.

____

2 Match the word to the meaning.

a Questionnaire   When you guide someone towards the answer you want

b Traffic   Cars, vans, buses – anything that drives on the road!

c Results   A question that has a specific answer

d Closed question   Something you ask somebody

e Questions   What you find out after carrying out a survey – your data

f Biased   A list of questions

3 Fill in the missing letters to make words about time.

a D _ _ _ _ _ _ _ _ sav _ _ _   d H _ _ r

b Gr _ _ _ w _ _ _   e T _ _ _ z _ _ _

c M _ _ _ dian   f _ l _ c _ _ _

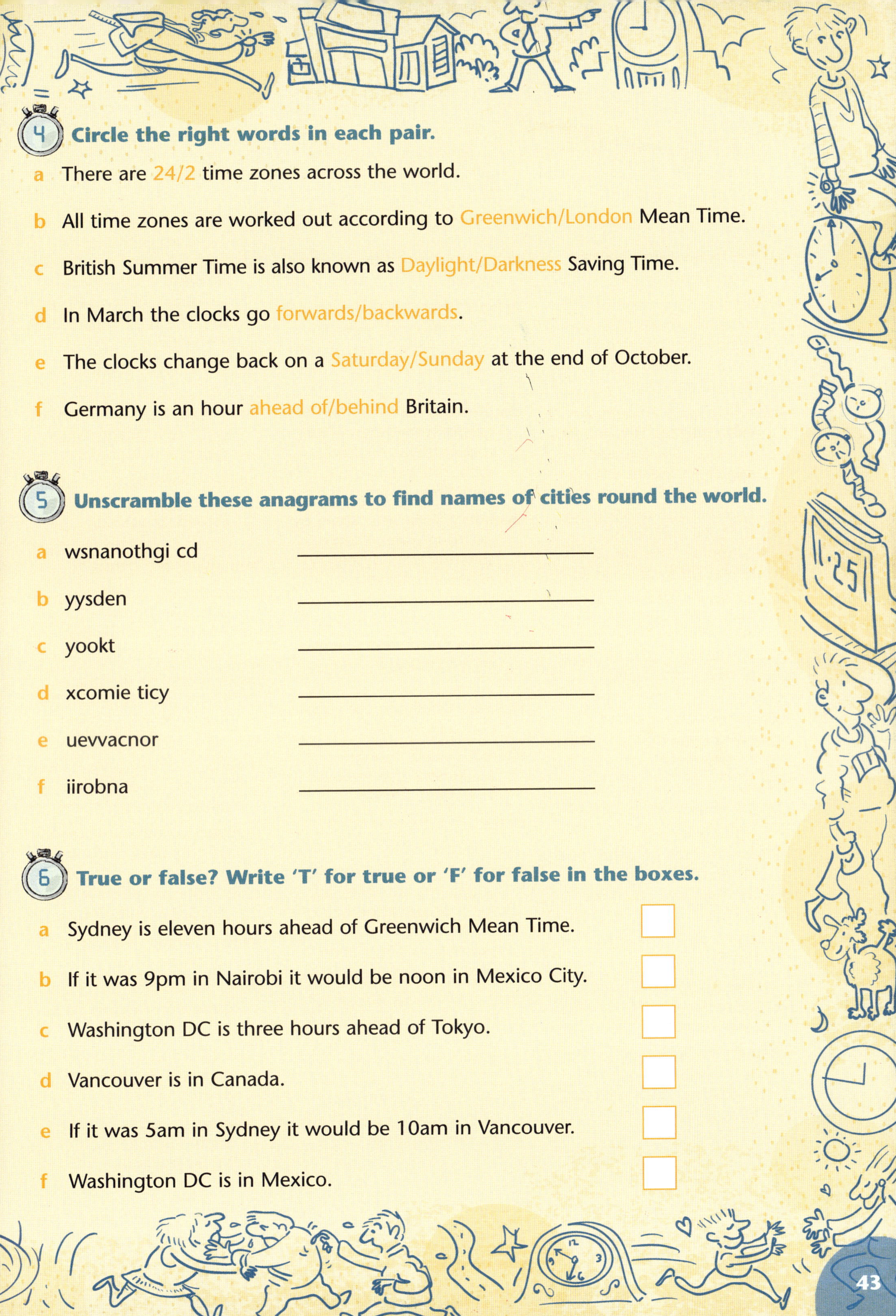

4 Circle the right words in each pair.

a There are 24/2 time zones across the world.

b All time zones are worked out according to Greenwich/London Mean Time.

c British Summer Time is also known as Daylight/Darkness Saving Time.

d In March the clocks go forwards/backwards.

e The clocks change back on a Saturday/Sunday at the end of October.

f Germany is an hour ahead of/behind Britain.

5 Unscramble these anagrams to find names of cities round the world.

a wsnanothgi cd _______________________

b yysden _______________________

c yookt _______________________

d xcomie ticy _______________________

e uevvacnor _______________________

f iirobna _______________________

6 True or false? Write 'T' for true or 'F' for false in the boxes.

a Sydney is eleven hours ahead of Greenwich Mean Time.

b If it was 9pm in Nairobi it would be noon in Mexico City.

c Washington DC is three hours ahead of Tokyo.

d Vancouver is in Canada.

e If it was 5am in Sydney it would be 10am in Vancouver.

f Washington DC is in Mexico.

Glossary

aquifer water-bearing rock formation

architecture a process of designing buildings. 'Victorian architecture' would be buildings from the Victorian age

average a usual amount; not extraordinary. In numbers (for example 'average rainfall') it means adding two or more quantities together and dividing by the total number of quantities. The average rainfall for a week would be all the daily rainfall quantities added together for seven days, and then divided by 7 (the number of days in the week)

biased showing a strong opinion about one side of an argument

bilharzia a disease caused by parasites found in infected water

border the area on either side of the dividing line between two countries

colliery a coal mine and buildings

colonies (of animals) groups of the same animals living close together

counties some countries, such as the UK, are divided into small areas called 'counties', for local government

dehydrated dried up; needing water

dengue fever a disease spread by mosquitoes. Infected people have a fever and pains in their joints

diarrhoea an illness spread by germs in the water. Waste matter leaves the body more often than usual, sometimes in liquid form

dysentery a disease caused by germs in water. People suffering from dysentery experience terrible, weakening diarrhoea

exit (of a motorway) the way off a motorway

facilities a building used for a particular activity

filtered passed through equipment that removes unwanted solids

flukes parasites that infect animals and people

food chain the way animals and plants are linked by the transfer of energy from one to another. An example would be: sun ➜ plant ➜ caterpillar ➜ bird

friction when two things rub together, the force called friction is created. This slows down moving objects, and makes them come to a stop. It also warms the things that are rubbed together.

Greenwich Mean Time the time meridian at Greenwich, in London; used for calculating the time in other parts of the world

gully a ditch or channel

household a group of people (such as a family) living together in a house

hygiene keeping clean and so avoiding certain illnesses caused by bacteria

impurities dirt; germs

industry the manufacturing of goods and/or the processing of raw materials in factories

infant mortality the rate at which young children die due to illness, accident etc.

malaria a serious illness carried by mosquitoes. Malaria causes fevers and chills

meridian a line on the globe which passes through a certain place on the earth's surface and also the North and South Poles

miners people who dig coal out of the earth

mines large holes deep in the ground for digging out coal

mosquitoes flying insects that suck blood and can infect people with diseases such as malaria

motorway a large, busy and important road such as the M1 in England

nightlife entertainment available at night, such as nightclubs, theatre etc.

parasites plants or creatures that live on or in another living thing. Parasites get energy from the creature or plant they live on

parasitic living on or in another thing

pedestrian a person on foot

pedestrianisation when an area is changed so that it is for people on foot only; no cars are allowed

penguin a black and white seabird in the Antarctic which uses its wings as flippers for swimming

pesticides chemicals used to kill pests on plants

pit closures when mines (pits) close down and no more coal is extracted from the ground

pits coal mines

polar ice caps permanent ice covering parts of the North and South Poles

quayside an area next to a river

questionnaire a list of questions used to find out information

recreation fun, relaxing activities

restored put back to its original state

roundworms parasites that live in the intestines of humans and animals

rural in the country

sanitation keeping people healthy with clean water and rubbish and waste collection

seams (of coal) where a layer of coal is found inside rock

sediment solids that settle at the bottom of a liquid

seed coat the outside layer of a seed that protects the inside

service station a place on a motorway or road where you can get food, drinks and go to the bathroom

sewers big underground pipes that carry water and waste away from cities, towns and villages for treatment

shipyards places where ships are built and mended

sleeping sickness a disease spread by tsetse flies. Infected people have fevers, shake and feel weak and sleepy

springs natural water that bubbles up out of the ground

survey collecting information about something by asking a set of questions

tapeworms large parasites that live in the intestines of infected humans and animals

time zone different places in the world have different times – they are in different 'time zones'. This can be ahead of or behind Greenwich Mean Time

traffic cars, buses, lorries etc.

tsetse flies bloodsucking flies that cause sleeping sickness and other illnesses when they bite people and animals

unemployment when people are unable to get a job

wagon way a route taken by wagons. In the past this could mean a special roadway for transporting coal wagons, which were pulled by horses

water-borne found in water

water cycle the way water evaporates, falls as rain and collects again in streams, rivers etc and returns to the sea – where it evaporates and the cycle starts again

yellow fever a disease caused by a virus that is spread by mosquitoes. Infected people suffer from jaundice, fever and vomiting

Answers

Page 5

Page 7

Line from 1950 to shipbuilding and pits

Line from 2005 to call centres, shop work and party city

Page 9

Many answers are appropriate. An example is:

There are many reasons to visit Newcastle. There is the exciting, vibrant quayside where you can visit the contemporary art centre – The Baltic – or if music is your thing there is also the new music centre, The Sage. If you fancy watching a game of football there is also the legendary St. James' Park, where Newcastle United play.

Pages 10–11 Revision exercises

Exercise 1

a F

b F

c T

d T

e T

f T

Exercise 2

a Newcastle

b London

c Leeds

d Wales

e Scotland

f Pennines

Exercise 3

a grim

b miners

c pits

d unemployment

e Newcastle

f closed

Exercise 4

a There were many mines and lots of industry and people only saw pictures of these things in papers when they heard about Newcastle

b They were miners and shipbuilders

c In the 1980s, because pits and shipyards closed

d They do all sorts of jobs, the same as anywhere else – for example, doctors, solicitors, teachers, etc – but there are many more 'service' jobs such as working in catering, bars and shops. There are also factories and new call centres

Exercise 5

a Grey Street

b Theatre Royal

c The Sage

d Baltic

e Quayside

f Tyne Bridge

Exercise 6

a St. James' Park

b Millennium Bridge

c The Baltic

d Seven Stories

e The quayside

Page 13

Across

3 Durham

4 council

5 colliery

Down

1 seams

2 drift mine

Page 15

Page 17

Pages 18–19 Revision exercises

Exercise 1

a T
b F
c T
d F
e T
f T

Exercise 2

a miner
b seams
c colliery
d coalfields
e mining works
f drift mine

Exercise 3

a Baltic
b facilities
c beaches
d Millennium
e Sage
f restaurants, bars

Exercise 4

a Restaurants
b Theatres
c Millennium Bridge
d Nightlife
e Bars
f River Tyne

Exercise 5

a People walking about; not in cars or other vehicles

b A road where cars cannot drive, but people can walk

c The Local Highway Authorities

d There are a several answers, such as: to protect historical environments; to make moving about safer for pedestrians

e There may be several answers; an example is: Northumberland Street

Exercise 6

a safer for pedestrians

b less pollution

c the extra walking keeps people fit

d harder for customers in cars to get close to shops; they may shop elsewhere

e cars have to go further to get to where they want to go

Page 21

```
s  l  l  e  w  v  d  a  g  e  h
s  o  e  g  n  a  g  l  r  g  g
b  o  c  b  t  r  l  a  s  a  m
e  u  i  e  r  o  w  t  i  l  r
t  n  a  r  a  a  b  s  e  l  e
b  e  b  a  l  n  o  a  k  o  f
r  e  i  c  a  l  g  i  d  n  i
r  a  c  i  l  i  t  d  e  s  u
b  r  a  v  c  n  t  i  o  y  q
p  o  l  a  r  n  t  i  o  t  a
```

Page 23

1 water
2 human
3 grow
4 depend
5 food chain
6 twenty litres
7 drink
8 plant
9 three days

Page 25

sprinklers

Pages 26–27 Revision exercises

Exercise 1

70, 326, 98, 2, 0.036

Exercise 2

a Aquifers
b Wells
c Glaciers
d Oceans
e Lakes
f Polar ice caps

Exercise 3

a F
b F
c F
d F
e T
f T

Exercise 4

a Twenty litres

b Water

c Wilt, then die

d Three days

e 65%

f No, because the creatures that eat other creatures (carnivores) would have nothing to eat as the plant eaters (herbivores) died out. They would die out because there would be no plants to eat. Plants also produce oxygen, which creatures need to breathe.

Exercise 5

Circled: dishwasher, washing machine, bath, sink and human

Exercise 6

a bath
b ice cube
c skiing
d dishwasher
e swimming
f washing machine

Page 29

Across

3 purified
4 aquifers

Down

1 chlorine
2 rural
3 polluted

Lines between 1 and Typhoid, Diarrhoea, Cholera, Polio and Meningitis

Lines between 2 and Bilharzia

Lines between 3 and Yellow fever, Sleeping sickness, Dengue fever, Malaria

Lines between 4 and Tuberculosis

Page 33

nobody owns water

Pages 34–35 Revision exercises

Exercise 1

a T	c F	e T
b F	d T	f T

Exercise 2

a Polluted	d Treatment
b Disinfected	e Sediment
c Chlorine	f Impurities

Exercise 3

a roundworm	d scarce
b polio	e billion
c malaria	f parasitic

Exercise 4

a Water Aid, Tearfund

b 3–4 million

c 1.2 billion

d Any 2 from the following: cholera, typhoid, polio, meningitis, diarrhoea

e a creature or plant that gets energy from another creature or plant it lives on and feeds off

f water can become polluted by chemical, human and animal waste

Exercise 5

a nobody	d gully
b Kenya	e 50,000
c water point	f 348

Exercise 6

a Nairobi	d slums
b sewage	e waste
c Kenya	f water point

Page 37

1 walk

2 bike

3 less than $\frac{1}{2}$ a mile

4 between 10 and 15 minutes

5 walk

Page 39

1 meridian	6 October
2 time zone	7 earlier
3 Greenwich	8 forwards
4 summer time	9 backwards
5 March	

Page 41

1 4am on Sunday	4 10am on Saturday
2 1pm on Saturday	5 12 noon on Saturday
3 9pm on Saturday	6 3am on Sunday

Pages 42–43 Revision exercises

Exercise 1

a Make sure you do not design questions that push people towards the answer you want or expect them to give.

b Closed

c Biased – trying to prove a point of view

d Many answers are possible, such as: favourite biscuits; routes to work/school; favourite hobbies etc.

e Write questions with specific answers. Don't make the questionnaire too long or people may get bored. Limit the amount of different choices you offer or it will be hard to find any 'results' – as everyone may have chosen a different answer.

Exercise 2

a A list of questions

b Cars, vans, buses – anything that drives on the road!

c What you find out after carrying out a survey – your data

d A question that has a specific answer

e Something you ask somebody

f When you guide someone towards the answer you want

Exercise 3

a Daylight saving	d Hour
b Greenwich	e Time zone
c Meridian	f Clocks

Exercise 4

a 24	d forwards
b Greenwich	e Sunday
c Daylight	f ahead of

Exercise 5

a Washington DC	d Mexico City
b Sydney	e Vancouver
c Tokyo	f Nairobi

Exercise 6

a F	c F	e F
b T	d T	f F